Can Archaeology Prove the New Testament?

Ralph O. Muncaster

HARVEST HOUSE PUBLISHERS
Eugene, Oregon 97402

Cover by Terry Dugan Design, Minneapolis, Minnesota

Special thanks to: Dr. Nancy Heidebrecht, professor of archaeology at Vanguard University and president of the Middle East Study Center; and Dr. Rex Moody, archaeological researcher, for their help in reviewing archaeological evidence and findings.

By Ralph O. Muncaster

Are There Hidden Codes in the Bible?
Can You Trust the Bible?
Can Archaeology Prove the New Testament?
Can Archaeology Prove the Old Testament?
Creation vs. Evolution
Creation vs. Evolution Video
Does the Bible Predict the Future?
How Do We Know Jesus Is God?
Is the Bible Really a Message from God?
Science—Was the Bible Ahead of Its Time?
What Is the Proof for the Resurrection?
What Really Happened Christmas Morning?
What Really Happens When You Die?

CAN ARCHAEOLOGY PROVE THE NEW TESTAMENT?
Copyright © 2000 by Ralph O. Muncaster
Published by Harvest House Publishers
Eugene, Oregon 97402

Library of Congress Cataloging-in-Publication Data

Muncaster, Ralph O.
    Can archaeology prove the New Testament? / Ralph O. Muncaster.
        p. cm. — (Examine the evidence series)
    Includes bibliographical references.
    ISBN 0-7369-0367-4
        1. Bible. N.T.—Evidences, authority, etc. 2. Bible. N.T.—Antiquities. 3. Jesus Christ—Historicity. I. Title.

BS2332 .M86 2000
225.9'3—dc21   00-039550

00 01 02 03 04 05 06 07 08 09 / BP / 10 9 8 7 6 5 4 3 2 1

Contents

What If "The Stones Could Talk"?

In a sense, they can.

The Bible presents itself as factual—historically and intellectually—and even as the only divinely inspired written work. It also commands us to test it (along with other supposed holy books) to know what is *really from God* (1 Thessalonians 5:21). New Testament archaeology plays a vital role in such a test by using stones, pottery, and other artifacts and features to tell us about the past.

Testing for divine inspiration requires much more than simply digging up what civilizations have left behind. It requires proof of the involvement of the supernatural. It requires evidence that only a God who knows the future with complete accuracy could provide. Prophecy is such a proof. And the Bible has lots of it— 668 historical prophecies in all. No other holy book has anything even remotely close to this.

> Archaeology supports prophecy
> with historical facts—
> and proves that prophecies were not fabricated
> (see page 14).

Archaeology and prophecy *together* help us know the Bible is from God. Archaeology helps validate the record of historical events in the Bible and also the reliability of the prophecies. And *perfectly fulfilled* prophecies provide statistical evidence that God must have inspired them in the first place.

Take, for instance, the 300-plus prophecies about Jesus. Of these, more and more of the historical ones are supported by the growing body of findings from New Testament archaeology. The odds of these prophecies being fulfilled in any *one* human being are about equal to the odds of winning 14 consecutive lotteries with the purchase of only 14 tickets. Put another way, if all the atoms in the entire universe were broken down into all their subparticles (electrons, protons, neutrons, and others), the odds of the prophecies of Jesus coming true in any one man would be like the odds of correctly selecting a single predesignated subatomic particle out of the entire contents of the universe.

If the Bible is what it says it is, then what it says is the most important information any human being could possibly seek. After all, it's from the God of the universe. The Bible describes the peace that can be achieved here on earth and the eternal paradise for all who believe and accept Him. It also describes the horrors of rejecting Him (and not accepting Him is rejection). Doesn't it make sense to take a few minutes to investigate the most important book of all time?

The Key Issues

The Foundational Issue of the New Testament:

Did the ministry, death, and resurrection of Jesus happen as recorded?

1. Can Historical Events Be Proven?

No.

As in a courtroom trial, the evidence must be evaluated.

Every day our legal system decides whether historical events—events now in the past—are true. Trial by jury provides a system to ascertain the occurrence of past events "beyond a shadow of a doubt." The "jury" of the New Testament consisted of the people of that time who listened to the evidence in favor of the Gospels—and these men and women chose to *die* for their convictions.

2. How *Do* We Confirm History?

By evaluation of the evidence:

- Eyewitness testimony

- Verification of testimony

- Circumstantial evidence

Whether the events took place yesterday or 2000 years ago, we need to review the eyewitness testimony, verify its accuracy, and examine the circumstantial evidence.

3. Does the Evidence Support the New Testament?

Yes!

- Writings of eyewitnesses

- Archaeological verification

- Other archaeological evidence

all confirm the New Testament record.

Eyewitnesses to the events of Jesus' life faced certain suffering and death to tell the truth. How many eyewitnesses in a court of law would do that today? Archaeology has verified the accounts of the eyewitnesses and has introduced circumstantial evidence to support the claims made in the New Testament.

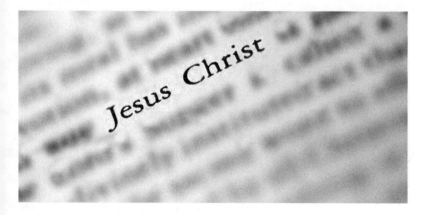

How the Bible Fits with History

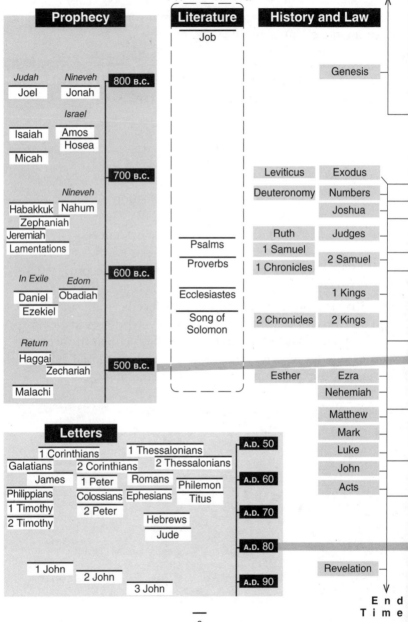

(Approximate Timing)

Prophecy | **Literature** | **History and Law** | C r e a t i

Creati

Prophecy

Judah — Joel
Nineveh — Jonah
800 B.C.
Israel
Isaiah
Amos
Hosea
Micah
700 B.C.
Nineveh
Habakkuk — Nahum
Zephaniah
Jeremiah
Lamentations
600 B.C.
In Exile — Daniel
Edom — Obadiah
Ezekiel
Return
Haggai
Zechariah
500 B.C.
Malachi

Literature

Job
Psalms
Proverbs
Ecclesiastes
Song of Solomon

History and Law

Genesis
Leviticus | Exodus
Deuteronomy | Numbers
Joshua
Ruth | Judges
1 Samuel
1 Chronicles | 2 Samuel
1 Kings
2 Chronicles | 2 Kings
Esther | Ezra
Nehemiah
Matthew
Mark
Luke
John
Acts
Revelation

Letters

1 Corinthians
Galatians
2 Corinthians
1 Thessalonians
2 Thessalonians
James
1 Peter
Romans
Philemon
Philippians
Colossians
Ephesians
Titus
1 Timothy
2 Peter
2 Timothy
Hebrews
Jude
1 John
2 John
3 John

A.D. 50
A.D. 60
A.D. 70
A.D. 80
A.D. 90

E n d
T i m e

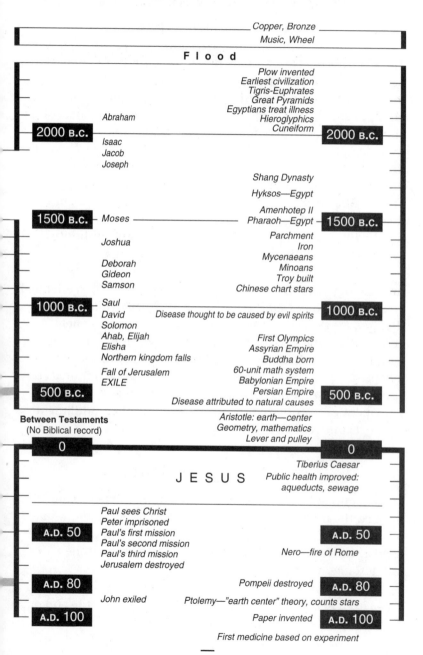

Copper, Bronze
Music, Wheel

F l o o d

Plow invented
Earliest civilization
Tigris-Euphrates
Great Pyramids
Egyptians treat illness
Hieroglyphics
Cuneiform

Abraham

2000 B.C. | **2000 B.C.**

Isaac
Jacob
Joseph

Shang Dynasty

Hyksos—Egypt

Amenhotep II

1500 B.C. Moses — Pharaoh—Egypt — **1500 B.C.**

Joshua | Parchment
Iron
Deborah | Mycenaeans
Gideon | Minoans
Samson | Troy built
Chinese chart stars

1000 B.C. Saul | **1000 B.C.**
David | Disease thought to be caused by evil spirits
Solomon
Ahab, Elijah | First Olympics
Elisha | Assyrian Empire
Northern kingdom falls | Buddha born
| 60-unit math system
Fall of Jerusalem | Babylonian Empire
EXILE | Persian Empire
500 B.C. | **500 B.C.**
Disease attributed to natural causes

Between Testaments | Aristotle: earth—center
(No Biblical record) | Geometry, mathematics
0 | Lever and pulley | **0**

Tiberius Caesar
J E S U S | Public health improved:
aqueducts, sewage

Paul sees Christ
Peter imprisoned
A.D. 50 Paul's first mission | **A.D. 50**
Paul's second mission
Paul's third mission | Nero—fire of Rome
Jerusalem destroyed

A.D. 80 | Pompeii destroyed | **A.D. 80**
John exiled | Ptolemy—"earth center" theory, counts stars

A.D. 100 | Paper invented | **A.D. 100**

First medicine based on experiment

9

New Testament History and Archaeology

The stage for the New Testament had been set throughout the period of the Old Testament. God's expectations were *defined* by the law of Moses in the first five books of the Bible. God's expectations were *clarified* through human example when Israel often chose to disobey the commandments of God. Mankind's need for redemption was stressed through a sacrificial system requiring shed blood for the cleansing of sin. Details of ceremonies, life-style, and even the building of holy structures were provided. The specific promise of a coming Messiah was reiterated in hundreds of prophecies throughout holy Scripture. When the Messiah finally did arrive, the Old Testament was the authority used to verify Jesus' fulfillment of these prophecies.

Archaeology helps us confirm the accuracy of the Old Testament (as summarized in *Can Archaeology Prove the Old Testament?* in the *Examine the Evidence* series). Likewise, archaeology helps verify the accuracy of the New Testament writings. Just as important, it can demonstrate the fulfillment of many of the incredibly precise prophecies about Jesus that took place hundreds of years after the prophecies were written. And finally, the New Testament can verify that the prophecies and their fulfillment were *not* contrived after the fact.

Intertestament History

From about 430 B.C. to the birth of Christ, the Bible is silent (this is called the intertestament period). The New Testament resumes the Bible's historical account just prior to the birth of John the Baptist. Other documents help provide the history of the intertestament period.

Persia exercised political control over Palestine from the end of the Jewish exile in the late 500s B.C. until Alexander the Great started his mighty campaign that resulted in the conquest of a vast region extending from India to Macedonia to Egypt, with the conquest of Palestine occurring in 334 B.C. Many archaeological findings confirm Alexander's influence.

The impact of Greece in this period far outlasted Alexander's control. In addition to many cultural changes, the common language of Palestine became *Koine* Greek—the language used to write most of the New Testament. Greek quickly became a universal language, as English is today. Many Jews became accustomed to speaking Greek and lost the ability to understand Hebrew. Hence the Scripture was translated from Hebrew into Greek in about 250 B.C. (the translation is called the *Septuagint*).

After Alexander's death in 323 B.C., struggles over Palestine occurred between the Seleucids, who ruled from Syria, and the Ptolemies, who ruled in Egypt. Eventually the hated Seleucid king Antiochus IV Epiphanes was defeated in the Maccabean revolt in 165 B.C. This led to a period of Jewish rule by the Hasmonean dynasty until the Romans finally seized control in 32 B.C. The area is rich in archaeological finds from this era.

The Gospel Accounts of Jesus

The four Gospels (Matthew, Mark, Luke, and John) summarize the period of history from about 2 B.C. to about A.D. 33. The events leading to the birth of John the Baptist, the forerunner of Jesus, are the first to be mentioned. Next, the events surrounding the birth of Jesus are recounted. But the vast majority of the Gospels deals with the three-and-a-half-year ministry of Jesus. About one-third of the Gospel accounts is devoted to the last week of His life.

The birth and death of Jesus took place in the area surrounding Jerusalem. This area is rich in archaeological finds, including the exact sites thought to be the actual places of the birth, death, and burial of Jesus. In addition, buildings, artifacts, and other findings help give light to and support the accounts of Jesus' activities in this region.

Jesus' ministry was centered in the region of Galilee. Several cities and areas are mentioned by name in the Gospel accounts and have been identified by archaeology. The many finds provide corroboration of the claims of the Gospel and also yield insight into the culture of the time of Jesus' teaching.

Although Jesus seldom traveled outside of Galilee, the detailed information contained in the accounts of His occasional trips to other portions of Palestine (for example, Judea) or Gentile regions (for example, Tyre and Sidon) is also supported by archaeology.

The Acts of the Apostles

The book of Acts was written by Luke as a historical extension of his book, the Gospel of Luke. It records the activities (acts) of the apostles following the resurrection of Jesus until almost A.D. 64. It is rich in historical detail and lends itself to verification by archaeology, which has confirmed the existence of most of the cities mentioned in the book and uncovered evidence of many people and events.

Acts outlines the formation of the early church. Beginning with the addition of a replacement disciple for Judas Iscariot, it continues with the anointing of the early church by the Holy Spirit at Pentecost. Evangelical speeches, vast conversions to Jesus, and severe persecution quickly followed Pentecost. A vital historical event occurred when Saul (Paul), a chief persecutor of the early Christians and a Pharisee, abruptly changed into a devout follower of Jesus upon seeing and hearing the risen Lord. The remainder of Acts summarizes the development of new churches, which was led to a significant degree by Paul, who wrote more of the New Testament than anyone else.

The Letters and Revelation

Letters written by the apostles (Paul, Peter, James, and others) were generally to help guide local churches in the teachings of Jesus. Hence they contain little historical information that can be tested, other than the names of the cities where the churches were built. Paul wrote the majority of these letters.

Revelation focuses on the end of time rather than history. Hence it also contains little historical information other than the cities and places that are mentioned.

Archaeology Verifies God's Input

The Ultimate Test of God

How do we know God exists? Literally, it's impossible to prove God's existence. On the other hand, it's impossible to prove *anything*. We don't know whether we'll be alive the next minute. We don't know whether our telephone will work for the next call. We don't know whether the next plane we take will lift off the ground. All of these things will *probably* happen, and we live as if they will. And all of them depend on something we don't see (spirit, electricity, and air). Nonetheless we believe.

We live our daily lives—each minute—
based on probability.

God tells us to use *prophecy* to test whether something is from Him (Deuteronomy 18:22). And prophecy is a *probability-based test*. In other words, if we prophesy that the sun will rise tomorrow, it doesn't mean much, since this is very probable. But if we were to prophesy that a man named "Ingledunk Herkanus" would win the U.S. presidency 500 years from now, and it proved true, it would be quite an amazing prophecy. Making dozens (or hundreds) of such prophecies, none wrong, would imply God's input.

The Bible contains 668 *historical* prophecies, and *none* have been shown false. Biblical prophecies are as specific and amazing as the hypothetical example above. Names of people, exact dates, places, and events have all been foretold in the Bible hundreds of years in advance. No other holy book has any significant historical (that is, provable) prophecy. God selected the prophecy test because only He can fulfill it. (If anything else could foretell the future, gambling wouldn't exist.)

Archaeology Verifies the Reliability of the Bible

Many of the Old Testament prophecies are about Jesus. The New Testament reveals their exact fulfillment hundreds of years after they were written. The odds of these prophecies coming true in one man by "accident" is one chance in—

10,000,000,000,000,000,000,000,000,000,000,000,000,000,000,000, 000,000,000,000,000,000,000,000,000,000,000,000,000,000,000.[1]

This would be like the chance of winning *14 consecutive lotteries with only 1 ticket for each.* Clearly impossible—without God. But how do we know the prophecies were actually written before the time of Jesus?

The *Dead Sea scrolls* provide proof that the prophecies of the Old Testament remained unchanged for 2000 years. In A.D. 70 the Essenes (a sect of Jews) sealed the caves of their libraries to protect them from the conquering Romans. The caves remained unentered until 1947, when the vast libraries were discovered. The scrolls had remained untouched for almost 2000 years—as with a time capsule.

The scrolls contain every book of the Old Testament except Esther, with multiple copies of most books. A large proportion of the scrolls were written well before the time of Jesus, some dating to almost 300 years earlier. When compared to the modern Hebrew Bible, virtually every letter of the scrolls agreed with the modern text. For 2000 years the Old Testament had remained unchanged—and the prophecies had also remained untouched and unchanged.

Archaeology—a New Science

It's natural to think of archaeology as an "old science." After all, it involves old things. Most people are surprised to learn that archaeology is relatively new.

Archaeology is the systematic study of things that past cultures have left behind. It was not a subject of professional interest until the 1700s. At that time it focused primarily on "valuable" objects (mainly gold and silver artifacts). The systematic (scientific*) approach wasn't widely used until the 1900s—years after some critics blindly—and incorrectly—assumed the Bible lacked any evidence to support it. In the late 1800s, "higher criticism" (popular at the time) suggested the Bible might be full of myths and errors. Some archaeologists sought to "prove" the Bible to be inaccurate. Others took the opposite approach and attempted to find evidence for it. The Bible archaeologists working in the Middle East were surprised at their discoveries, which supported the Bible in virtually all details (see insert on "Great Archaeologists"). Some other archaeologists who searched the Americas for evidence of other holy books (for example, the *Book of Mormon,* written in the 1800s), found no evidence and began refocusing on early American Indian cultures.

Using the Bible as a guide, archaeologists began finding parts of history they didn't know existed. Ancient cultures thought to be nonexistent were discovered. Ancient cities thought to be myths were found. And events thought to be legends were confirmed. Today the Bible is regarded as a fundamental archaeological reference.

* Some people define "science" as only those disciplines using the scientific method. Others broaden it to include almost all areas of systematic fact finding.

We should realize, however, that most of this archaeological evidence has appeared in the *last 50 years*. Only since half a century ago have discoveries led to confirmation of the existence of cities such as Sodom and Gomorrah, people as prominent as King David, or cultures such as the early Hittites. Now museums are filled with archaeological evidence supporting the Bible. Yet many textbooks and much public opinion is still based on remnants of the inaccurate period of "higher criticism" from the 1800s to the early 1900s. Unfortunately, it takes time to correct long-standing misconceptions.

Great Archaeologists Switch to the Bible

Old Testament: *William Albright*—As a young man, Albright regarded the Bible as simply a book of literature not based on historical fact. He intended to use archaeology to define how such "literature" fit within the cultural framework of its time. During his field studies in the 1930s (which continued until his death in 1971), Albright found conclusive evidence that caused him to reverse his previous position. He proclaimed that the Bible was, in fact, *totally consistent with archaeological findings*.

New Testament: *William Ramsay*—Ramsay set out to disprove Luke in the late nineteenth century. After 30 years of in-depth archaeology in Asia Minor and the Middle East, Ramsay's conclusions were the opposite of his initial premise. The academic world was shocked. Expecting historical proof against the Bible, instead it was presented with strong confirmation of biblical accuracy. Ramsay called Luke one of the greatest historians ever—and he converted to Christianity based on his research.

How Archaeology Is Conducted

Modern archaeology is highly organized and meticulous, keeps records in depth, and is *very* slow. Centuries ago "treasure hunters" obliterated many sites in search of quick riches. Today, archaeologists value most writings and artifacts more than gold or gems.

In the Middle East, the common form of a site for excavation is a large mound, called a *tell*, which is essentially a buried city. Tells usually span several cultures. Throughout history, building sites were carefully selected based on such things as water supply, food sources, and natural defenses. When a city was conquered and destroyed, it was typical for the victors to rebuild on top of the old city. As time passed, this cycle of destruction and rebuilding resulted in a large man-made hill. Of course, the uppermost level represented the most recent civilization, the lower ones earlier cultures. Occasionally pits were dug through several strata by the residents.

As excavation takes place, the precise location and relationship of various artifacts are lost forever. Therefore, digs are systematically divided into square areas and frequently photographed. Each artifact is thoroughly documented. Digging may start with shovels, which, as critical areas are approached, are quickly replaced with small hand tools—even spoons and toothbrushes. Because of the enormous time and expense required, only a small dent has been made to date in the tens of thousands of potential sites.

How Archaeological Dates Are Determined

Seldom do people leave behind inscriptions of dates or valuable dated materials, such as coins. However, the vast amount of pottery left behind—with obvious style changes that can be referenced to dates—provides an abundant and reliable source of dating. As an example, the oil lamps below show a very distinct progression of style readily recognizable by archaeologists. Such lamps are very commonly found in the Holy Lands.[2]

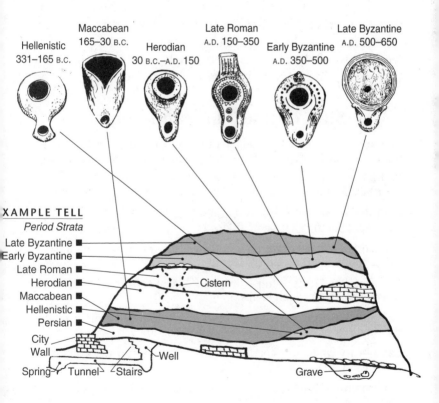

Hellenistic
331–165 B.C.

Maccabean
165–30 B.C.

Herodian
30 B.C.–A.D. 150

Late Roman
A.D. 150–350

Early Byzantine
A.D. 350–500

Late Byzantine
A.D. 500–650

XAMPLE TELL
Period Strata

Late Byzantine
Early Byzantine
Late Roman
Herodian
Maccabean
Hellenistic
Persian

City
Wall

Spring Tunnel Stairs

Well

Cistern

Grave

The Sites of Jesus' Life and Ministry

The vast majority of Jesus' time was spent in the region of Galilee. Yet His influence was felt throughout the region. Jesus visited the Gentile areas of Tyre and Sidon (Matthew 15:21), the Transjordan area (the area east of the Jordan, also heavily Gentile), Samaria (John 4:5), and a few selected cities near Jerusalem in Judea.

Also, many people, including religious leaders, came to see Him. We know that "many people came to him from Judea, Jerusalem, Idumea, and the regions across the Jordan and around Tyre and Sidon" (Mark 3:8). This was an extensive travel commitment in ancient times. The trip from Jerusalem to Nazareth took about 4 to 5 days. Travel from areas further south (for example, Idumea) took several days longer. And there was no schedule—no guarantee Jesus would be in town when people arrived. All this shows that Jesus made an enormous impact on the region.

Sites of Jesus' Life and Ministry

Bethany—Site where Jesus apparently lived during His last week of ministry (Matthew 21:17). Jesus was anointed there (Matthew 26:6).

Bethlehem—Birthplace of Jesus (Matthew 2:1). Magi visited Jesus there (Matthew 2:9). Herod slaughtered children (Matthew 2:16).

Bethphage—Site where Jesus sent disciples to retrieve a donkey for His final entrance into Jerusalem (Mark 11:1).

Bethsaida—Village in which Jesus healed a blind man (Mark 8:22). Site where Jesus fed 5000 (Luke 9:10).

Caesarea (Maritima)—Important port. Site of conversion of centurion by Peter (Acts 10:1) and Paul's trial (Acts 23:33).

Caesarea Philippi—City where Peter first proclaimed Jesus as the Messiah, the son of the living God (Matthew 16:16).

Cana—City where Jesus performed first miracle—turning water into wine (John 2:1).

Capernaum—Headquarters of Jesus' ministry (Matthew 4:13). Many miracles performed. Home of Peter.

Emmaus—An early appearance of Jesus after the resurrection occurred on the road to this town (Luke 24:13).

Gennesaret—Jesus arrived here after calming the seas. People brought sick people to be healed by Jesus (Matthew 14:35).

Gadara—Demon-possessed man came from the region bearing this city's name (Luke 8:26).

Gergesa—Actual site on Sea of Galilee where the demon-possessed pigs ran down a steep bank into the sea (Matthew 8:28).

Jericho—Just outside of this city, Jesus healed blind Bartimaeus (Mark 10:46).

Jerusalem—Most important Jewish city. Site of temple. Jesus was crucified, buried, and resurrected there.

Magdala—Fishing village on the Sea of Galilee. Believed to be the home of Mary Magdalene.

Nain—Site where Jesus raised a widow's son from the dead (Luke 7:11).

Nazareth—Important trade crossroad. Home of Jesus during His youth. Site of limited number of miracles (Mark 6:5).

Sepphoris—Capital city of Herod Antipas. Very close to Nazareth. It's possible Jesus worked there as a carpenter.

Sidon—Important Mediterranean port city. Jesus visited to minister to Gentiles (Matthew 15:21).

Sychar—City in Samaria where Jesus met the woman at the well, promising her "living water" (John 4:5).

Tyre—Important Mediterranean port city. Jesus visited to minister to Gentiles (Matthew 15:21).

The Sites of Paul's Ministry

Paul's ministry had an enormous impact on the New Testament. While starting a vast network of churches, he wrote more books of the Bible than anyone else.

Sites of Paul's Ministry

Antioch (Pisidia)—Paul preached in synagogue and founded church there (Acts 13:14-49).

Antioch (Syria)—Base for missionary journeys of Paul and Barnabas (Acts 13:1-3;15:30-41; 18:22,23).

Assos—Roman seaport visited by Paul (Acts 20:13,14).

Athens—Capital of Greece, visited by Paul (Acts 17:15).

Berea—Paul preached here with great success (Acts 17:10).

Caesarea (Maritima)—Port of embarkation. Paul tried and imprisoned here until final trip to Rome (Acts 23:33).

Cenchrea—Paul sailed from this seaport (Acts 18:18).

Corinth—Most important trade center of Greece. Paul established influential, flourishing church (Acts 18:1-18).

Derbe—Refuge for Paul on two journeys (Acts 14:6; 16:1).

Ephesus—Large economic center where Paul established a prominent church (Acts 19:1; 20:16).

Iconium—Refuge of Paul and Barnabas after expulsion from Antioch, Pisidia (Acts 13:51).

Lystra—Refuge for Paul after Iconium. Home of Timothy (Acts 16:1). Paul stoned here (Acts 14:19).

Malta—Small island between Sicily and Africa, where Paul was shipwrecked (Acts 28:1).

Miletus—Seaport visited by Paul. Farewell message to elders of church of Ephesus there (Acts 20:15-38).

Mitylene—Wealthy island city visited by Paul (Acts 20:14).

Paphos—Paul, Barnabus, John Mark visited (Acts 13:6). Paul met Sergius Paulus, a believer (Acts 13:12).

Patara—Paul transferred ships to return to Tyre (Acts 21:1).

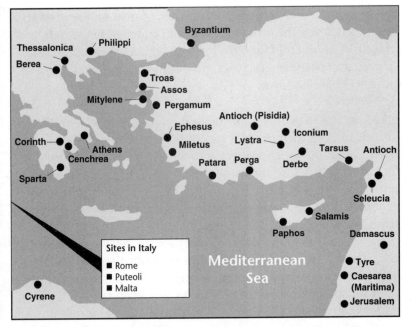

Pergamum—Site of one of Revelation's seven churches of Asia (Revelation 2:12).

Philippi—Historically important city where Paul started an important church (Acts 16:12; 20:6).

Puteoli—Grain shipping port visited by Paul (Acts 28:13).

Rome—Capital of Roman Empire. City where Paul was imprisoned, wrote letters, and possibly was martyred.

Salamis—Port city visited by Paul, Barnabas (Acts 13:5).

Seleucia—Seaport where Paul, Barnabas started first missionary journey (Acts 13:4).

Tarsus—Birthplace and refuge of Paul (Acts 21:39; 22:3).

Thessalonica—Visited by Paul, successful church established there (Acts 17:1).

Troas—Visited often by Paul. Saw vision of invitation to preach the gospel in Europe (Acts 16:8,9).

Historical Tradition

It's common to venerate important sites of history. For instance, Americans revere historical sites such as Independence Hall, Mount Vernon, and Lincoln's birthplace. If a catastrophe destroyed any of these structures, no doubt the sites would continue to be well known.

Likewise, the sites of New Testament archaeology were well known in their own time. First, nonbiblical historical documents *reveal a clear lineage of relatives of Christ extending into the third century.*[3] Relatives would know the sites of the birth and death of Jesus and of the important events of His life. Second, the followers of Jesus had an amazing passion for the truth of the gospel—a truth worthy of dying for. So it's not surprising that in spite of persecution many sites of the Gospel accounts were recorded in early church tradition. These traditions about sites are not always accurate, but when they are substantiated by early historians, their reliability is strengthened. Ironically, even the attempts to end reverence of those sites by erecting pagan memorials on them only served to mark the sites until the Roman Empire's acceptance of Christianity in the fourth century, after which the sites could be openly recognized.

Historical Tradition Versus Legend

How do we separate the legend of George Washington throwing a silver dollar across the wide Potomac from the tradition that Washington's home was at Mount Vernon? We can test the evidence by the following criteria:

1. Is there *early* evidence of *belief* in the place or event as historical fact?

2. Is the early evidence from a *reliable source*?

3. Is there early evidence that the place or event was *widely accepted* as fact?

Valid historical traditions can pass these tests, while legends can't. The reason is that *legends take time to develop into belief.* Obviously if a ridiculous statement is made (for example, that Elvis Presley rose from the dead), the contemporary audience will reject it as nonsense. Little documentation, if any, would survive, and there would be virtually no contemporary followers of the belief. *The opposite happened with the biblical events.* There was a *vast explosion* of belief *in spite of persecution* and attempts to eradicate those beliefs about the events surrounding Jesus. In the case of the ridiculous, only time can allow it to seem plausible. It took centuries for people to deify Buddha or Confucius (which, by the way, ran counter to their own teachings). As another instance, some people now deify Mary, Jesus' mother—many centuries after the fact. However, the sites and events surrounding *Jesus Himself* were quickly believed and recorded *by contemporaries.*

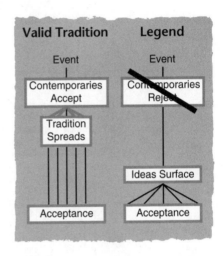

Archaeological Evidence of the New Testament

(A small sample of discoveries to date)

Some New Testament Archaeological Find

Before Jesus' Ministry

p.28 ✳ Site of the annunciation of Jesus' birth
p.28 ✳ Second site of annunciation
p.29 🏛 Birthplace of John the Baptist
p.29 🏛 Birthplace of Jesus
p.30 🏛 Joseph's house
p.31 ✳ Site of the baptism of Jesus
p.31 🏛 Cana—Jesus changes water into wine
p.31 🏛 Samaria—the woman at the well
p.32 🏛 Capernaum—Jesus' synagogue
p.33 🏛 Capernaum—Peter's house

KEY

👤 **People**—evidenc of people or grou

🏛 **Places**—evidenc of cities or sites

🅒 **Culture**—eviden of items or practi

✳ **Events**—evidenc of historical even

Jesus' Early Ministry

p.33 ✳ Feeding of the multitudes
p.34 🏛 Tax office of Matthew
p.34 ✳ Healing of the demoniacs—demons cast into pigs
p.34 🏛 Tomb of John the Baptist
p.35 🏛 Bethsaida—birthplace of some of the disciples
p.35 🅒 Fishing boat used on the Sea of Galilee
p.35 🏛 Magdala—birthplace of Mary Magdalene
p.35 🏛 Caesarea—Roman capital of Palestine
p.36 👤 Caesarea—evidence of Pontius Pilate
p.36 ✳ Caesarea—the praetorium where Paul was guarded
p.36 🏛 Other cities in northern Palestine

Jesus' Middle Ministry

p.36 🅒 Jericho—Herod's winter headquarters
p.37 👤 Jericho—tree of Zacchaeus
p.37 🏛 Jericho—the inn of the Good Samaritan
p.38 🏛 Bethany—the tomb of Lazarus
p.38 🏛 Bethphage—Jesus begins the final entry
p.39 🏛 Mount of Olives—Jesus reveals end-time events
p.39 ✳ Mount of Olives—Jesus weeps over the city
p.39 🏛 The temple in Jerusalem
p.40 🏛 The last supper
p.40 🏛 Gethsemane

Jesus' Later Ministry

p.40 🏛 Trials of Jesus—Caiaphas and Pilate
p.41 🏛 Site of Jesus' death and resurrection
p.41 🏛 The ascension of Jesus
p.42 ✳ Various languages spoken at Pentecost
p.42 🅒 Deception by Sapphira
p.42 🏛 Synagogue of the Freedmen
p.42 👤 Ethiopian eunuch
p.42 👤 Confirmation of the existence of Sergius Paulus

Church Expansion

p.43 ✳ John Mark's sudden return to Jerusalem
p.43 🅒 Correction of information about Iconium, Lystra, and Der
p.44 🅒 Confirmation of the "District" of Macedonia
p.44 🏛 Confirmation of the word "Rulers"
p.44 ✳ Paul's stay in Corinth
p.45 👤 Inscription naming Erastus
p.45 ✳ Dating of the book of Revelation

Jesus' Relatives Were in Nazareth

Nonbiblical sources reveal that relatives of Jesus resided in the area of Nazareth at least until the third century (and perhaps much longer). Julius Africanus (circa 200) writes of relatives of the Lord who came from both Nazareth and nearby Cochaba and who kept "records of their descent with great care."[3]

Eusebius (circa 300) writes of two grandsons of Jude, brother of Jesus, who were brought before the emperor Domitian in the fifteenth year of his reign (the year 95) and were freed when they admitted to being from the house of David. They then started several churches in the area "because they were relatives of the Lord." Eusebius also mentions Symeon, son of Clopas (who was thought to be Joseph's brother), who succeeded James as church leader and was martyred at the age of 120.[3]

Stones may not talk—but people do!

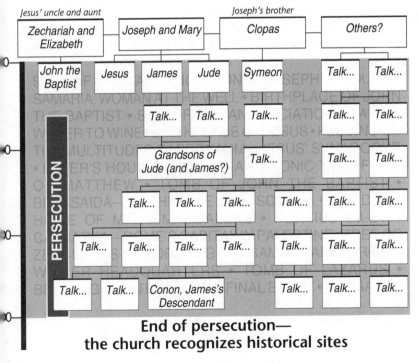

**End of persecution—
the church recognizes historical sites**

Ancient Discoveries—
The Time Before Jesus' Ministry

✹ **The Site of the Annunciation of Jesus' Birth**—Since relatives of Jesus lived in the Nazareth area well into the third century, we might expect the site of Mary's first encounter with the angel Gabriel to have been identified. The Church of the Annunciation (rebuilt in 1969) traditionally marks the place where the angel appeared to announce the birth of Jesus to Mary (Luke 1:26-38). Several earlier churches marked this same site, but were repeatedly destroyed, especially during the violent period of the Crusades. Excavation shows early veneration of the site, which can be dated back to the third century by architectural style and much early-period graffiti. In addition, foundations, walls, and detailed mosaics from other early churches were discovered.

Underneath the church are two grottos. The larger one is believed to be the actual place where Mary saw the angel (tradition says while "spinning scarlet thread"). It may have been a dwelling or possibly an underground storeroom common to the period. The grottos also contain elaborate floor mosaics. Since one mosaic contains a pattern of crosses that abruptly ceases, it was probably under construction in 427, when Emperor Theodosius II issued an edict forbidding the decoration of floors with the images of crosses. The second, smaller grotto has been identified as honoring the martyr Conon, a relative of Jesus (see insert on page 27), who was put to death around the year 250 in Asia Minor.[3]

✹ **The Second Site of Annunciation**—Careful reading of Luke 1:26-38 indicates there may have been two visitations of Mary by the Angel Gabriel—one in the town of Nazareth, perhaps by the town's spring (Luke 1:26-28), and a second in her dwelling (Luke 1:29-38). Daniel (in 1106) records the popular belief in two such appearances—the first at the spring and the second at Mary's house. He also mentions the construction of two churches, one to memorialize each site. Today, the Church of St. Gabriel stands beside the major water supply to Nazareth. The original outlet of the spring of the crypt, where the boy "Jesus would often draw water," is still visible today.[3]

P **The Birthplace of John the Baptist**—Zechariah and Elizabeth, John the Baptist's parents, lived in the hill country outside Jerusalem (Luke 1:65). A church marking the site of the birth of John the Baptist and the visit by Mary (Luke 1:39) was described in 940 by Eutychius. In 1106, Daniel also wrote about this church and indicated that a small cavern beneath the altar was the site where "John the Forerunner" was born. Today, the Church of St. John the Baptist (built in the eleventh century) stands over the original foundation of the early church that marked the site. Graves with pottery and coins dated to the time of John the Baptist were found.[3]

P **The Birthplace of Jesus**—The Church of the Nativity in Bethlehem marks the traditional spot of the birth of Jesus. The construction of the original church was ordered by Constantine's mother, Helena. (Constantine was the emperor who ended the persecution of Christians and made Christianity the official church of the Roman Empire). As with many Christian sites, attempts were made to stop the worship of Jesus by destroying this site; but an indication of restored worship—a church—always seemed to reappear. Excavation at the site of the Church of the Nativity reveals evidence of earlier churches, including columns and capitals actually dating to the time of Constantine. Early writers indicated that Jesus was born in a cave, which was a common site for a stable during that time. The exact location of the cave of Jesus' birth is thought to be under an altar that marks the spot in the present day Church of the Nativity.[1,3,4,5]

P **Joseph's House**—Joseph and Jesus were carpenters who lived in Nazareth (Matthew 13:55; Mark 6:3; Luke 4:16). Located only 100 meters from Mary's home is the site of the house of Joseph—where Jesus grew up—commemorated now by the Church of St. Joseph. As is typical with Christian memorials, churches were built and rebuilt on the site following successive attempts to destroy it. Archaeological evidence reveals a Crusader church built on top of an earlier Byzantine church, which had been built over two vaults identifying the house of Joseph. In addition to early writings describing this first church, Roman artifacts indicate habitation in the area at the time of Jesus.[3]

Ancient Discoveries—

The Time of Jesus' Early Ministry

The Site of the Baptism of Jesus—Jesus was baptized by John the Baptist in the lower Jordan river (Luke 3:3), where people from Jerusalem and Judea "went out to John" (Matthew 3:5,6; Mark 1:5). The Monastery of St. John stands near the site of Jesus' baptism, which would be at one of three places that were used to cross the river. All these sites are located within a few miles of each other, and all are also in the vicinity where Elijah preached. (Naturally there are many significant parallels between Elijah and John the Baptist.) The most probable of these three sites is located at Bethabara "on the banks of the Jordan," as indicated by third-century church father Origen.[3]

Cana: Jesus Changes Water into Wine—Jesus' first and second miracles after the beginning of His ministry were performed in Cana. First, while Jesus and His mother were attending a wedding feast, the hosts ran out of wine. After His mother told Him of the need, Jesus turned several jars of water into fine wine (John 2:1-11). Second, some while later an official travelled to Jesus' new hometown of Capernaum to request the healing of his son in Cana. Jesus granted his request without actually traveling there (John 4:46-54).

There is dispute between two ancient sites as to the actual location of Cana. Both have Roman artifacts from the time of Jesus. The smaller site, closer to Nazareth (Kefar Kenna) has a church commemorating the "miracle of the wine," which some believe is the church described by Williabald in 725. On the church altar is a jar that is said to be one of the six jars of Jesus' miracle. Others believe the unexcavated site of Khirbet Kana, nine miles from Nazareth (home of Josephus, the Jewish historian) is more likely. [3,5,6]

Samaria: The Woman at the Well—Soon after the events in Cana, Jesus went to Jerusalem, then journeyed back to Capernaum through Samaria—an area avoided by the Jews. Jesus met a woman at the well in Sychar that Jacob had built and displayed miraculous knowledge of her past sins. He offered her the "living water" of eternal life. Many of the people of Samaria became followers of Jesus (John 4:1-41).

The city of Sychar in Samaria (John 4:5) has been located about 35 miles north of Jerusalem, on Mount Gerizim. Ancient documents and the Madaba Mosaic refer to this location. The area contains Jacob's well, over which a medieval church was built. It now is memorialized by an unfinished Greek Orthodox monument. The well still produces water. Also in the area is the tomb of Joseph, who asked that his body be returned from Egypt (Genesis 50:25).[3,5]

P **Capernaum: Jesus' Synagogue**—Early in His ministry, Jesus made Capernaum His hometown. The city was the largest fishing center on the northern end of the Sea of Galilee. The Capernaum synagogue in which Jesus preached has been located underneath the ruins of later synagogues. The style of construction, materials used, and location all indicate an early-first-century origin. Excavation along the western wall revealed walls, pavement, household articles, and pottery of that same time. The lower-level floors that were excavated contained early pottery and a coin dated to about 146-116 B.C. (the reign of Ptolemy VIII of Egypt), indicating the synagogue's likely presence during Jesus' time.

Presumably Jesus spent much time in the synagogue. Of particular interest is the miracle Jesus performed for the centurion, who came to Jesus, perhaps at the synagogue, to ask Jesus to heal his servant (Matthew 8:5).[1,3,4,5,6]

Jesus' Brothers, Sisters, and Relatives

The Bible clearly distinguishes between Jesus' "blood" brothers and sisters and His disciples (Matthew 12:46-50). Archaeology reveals that the *early* Church of Rome acknowledged Jesus' relatives, including His brothers James and Jude, the grandsons of James and Jude, His cousin Symeon, and other descendant relatives such as Conon. Early documents, mosaics, inscriptions, and monuments all attest to this. The existence of Jesus' relatives was also confirmed by eye-witnesses and non-Christian historians.

Centuries later, the evolved Roman Catholic Church denied the same people it had earlier memorialized, after redefining Mary as a perpetual virgin.

Which is legend? Jesus' relatives or Mary's perpetual virginity?

P Capernaum: Peter's House—Excavation near the Capernaum synagogue reveals several dwellings. Of particular interest is one that has been revered for centuries as the house of Peter. The style of architecture precisely matches the type of home mentioned in the Bible, from which the roof was partially removed to let down a paralytic (Mark 2:4). In addition, the house is located close to the shore of the Sea of Galilee and even contains fishhooks on the floor. It was obviously the house of a fisherman.

Most important is the evidence that supports the long-standing tradition of the house being Peter's. Aetheria, a pilgrim in the area from 381–384, wrote about the existence of the house of the first of the apostles, "where the paralytic was healed." In addition, there is evidence that the site was venerated by many people from early in the Christian era. A substantial amount of early graffiti dating back to the second century have been found (124 fragments in Greek, 15 in Hebrew, and 18 in Syriac). The graffiti speak of the apostle Peter, of Jesus, and of requests for Jesus' help. The house of Peter was converted early into a place of worship and was significantly changed at least three times. The earliest evidence of its use as a place of worship dates back to the first century, a time contemporary with Peter.[1,3,4,5,6]

✸ The Feeding of the Multitudes with Five Loaves and Two Fish—A large crowd followed Jesus to a remote place to hear His teaching. Later, knowing that the crowd was hungry and without food, Jesus took five loaves of bread and two fish and miraculously multiplied them into enough food to feed 5000 people (Mark 6:32-44). Aetheria (see above) describes the site and a church that commemorated the amazing miracle as being at Seven Springs, a few miles from Capernaum. Excavation has uncovered the church, which contains an elaborate floor mosaic showing the loaves and fish in detail. An inscription just above the mosaic from the artist says, "In this holy place, Lord, remember Sauros."

The modern Church of the Multiplication of the Loaves and Fishes, built in the twentieth century, encloses the sites of previous churches that were destroyed by an earthquake and during Persian and Arab invasions.[3]

P **The Tax Office of Matthew**—The disciple and New Testament author Matthew was a tax collector (Matthew 9:9). The tax office would have certainly been on a major interregional highway. Such a site was identified by Aetheria as at Seven Springs, which was also said to be "near the walls of the church commemorating the feeding of the multitudes with five loaves and two fishes."[3]

The Healing of the Demoniacs: Demons Cast into Pigs—Jesus encountered two demon-possessed men who roamed the graves in the region of Gadara and were feared by everyone (Matthew 8:28-34). Jesus cast the demons out of the men and into a herd of pigs, which immediately "ran down a steep bank" and drowned in the Sea of Galilee.

This site has been identified with the town of Gergesa, located on the Sea of Galilee in the Gadara area. A steep slope leads into the lake. In the rocky hills above the lake are remains of Roman settlements and caves that fit the biblical description of an area of tombs. Ruins of an early church and monastery have been excavated. Also, around a massive boulder, there are remains of a large chamber with an adjoining tower. Experts believe the boulder may have been the site of Jesus' miracle, and the structure was built to commemorate it.[3]

P **The Tomb of John the Baptist**—John the Baptist was beheaded at the request of Salome, daughter of Herodias. The place of the beheading was in the remote, gloomy fortress of Machaerus across the Jordan. The disciples then buried the body (Matthew 14:12), probably in the long-venerated tomb now enclosed by the Church of John the Baptist at nearby Samaria-Sebaste.

A legend that John's head was buried in the Samaria-Sebaste Church of the Finding of the Head of John the Baptist persisted for centuries. Archaeology has now corrected that myth by finding evidence that the supposed palace of Herod—the church site—was actually a large temple built by Herod. The location of the church was in Pilate's jurisdiction, whereas Machaerus was in Herod's.[3]

Ancient Discoveries—
The Time of Jesus' Middle Ministry

P **Bethsaida: The Birthplace of Some of the Disciples**—Peter, Andrew, James, John, and Philip—almost half of the disciples—were born in the village of Bethsaida (according to writings of Theodosius, and John 1:44). One of two sites on the east side of the Jordan River near Capernaum is probably the actual site of the fishing village. One newly excavated site, et-Tell, contains pottery and a large ancient stone wall. The other site, at Khirbet el-Araj, contains traces of ancient buildings and mosaics.[3,4,5]

C **A Fishing Boat Used on the Sea of Galilee**—Near Bethsaida, a fishing boat used in the time of Christ was discovered. It was $26^1/2$ feet long, $7^1/2$ feet wide, and $4^1/2$ feet high. Originally it was equipped with a mast for sailing and had two sets of oars. Considering the smaller stature of people in Jesus' day, it could have accommodated up to 15 passengers. This was the type of boat that was probably used to cross of the Sea of Galilee, including the time Jesus calmed the storm (Matthew 8:23-27) and the time He walked on water (Matthew 14:22-33).[3,5]

P **Magdala: The Birthplace of Mary Magdalene**—Mary Magdalene became a close follower of Jesus after He cast seven demons out of her (Luke 8:2). Mary was with Jesus as He died on the cross and witnessed His burial and resurrection. Mary's name—Magdalene—literally means "the one from Magdala." Epiphanius wrote sometime between 750–800 of a church in Magdala that was known as the place where Jesus had cast out the seven demons. No remains of this church have been found yet. However, a synagogue has been excavated that contains coins and pottery from the time of Jesus. A Roman-period water tower also indicates a prospering village that was in existence prior to A.D. 70.[3]

P **Caesarea: The Roman Capital of Palestine**—The most important city and port of Roman Palestine was built by Herod the Great in honor of Caesar Augustus. The completion of Caesarea took about 12 years and was celebrated with a great festival. The city was especially important in Jesus' time. Paul returned to Caesarea on his second missionary journey (Acts 18:22). He also stood trial there before Felix, Festus, and Agrippa (Acts 24–26) and was imprisoned there before being shipped to Rome to stand trial.[3,4,5,6]

Caesarea: Evidence of Pontius Pilate Found—During the excavation of the Roman theater at Caesarea, a stone was found in the landing of a flight of steps. It bears the inscription "To the people of Caesarea Tiberium Pontius Pilate Prefect of Judea." Another line seems to indicate the word meaning "dedication." It is likely that the stone was originally placed on an outside wall to commemorate the theater's construction.[3,5]

Caesarea: The Praetorium Where Paul Was Guarded—The Promontory Palace used by Herod Agrippa and other prominent officials has been discovered. Inside it is an elaborate floor mosaic that is probably part of the areas where Paul was guarded (Acts 23:35).[3]

Other Cities in Northern Palestine—Several other cities in northern Palestine are mentioned in the New Testament. Among them are places Jesus visited, including Tyre, Sidon, and some of the ten cities of the Decapolis. There are others that probably were visited by Jesus. A good example is Sepphoris, which was being built as a capital city for Herod Antipas during Jesus' youth (the capital was later moved to Tiberius on the Sea of Galilee). Since Sepphoris was only two miles from Nazareth, and since the work of carpenters included stonemasonry, it's quite likely Jesus and His father were involved in the city's construction. Among the cities that Jesus may never have visited are Caesarea Philippi and Chorazin. In most cases, city excavations have been underway. [3,5,6]

Jericho: Herod's Winter Headquarters—New Testament Jericho was located at a nearby but different location from Old Testament Jericho. For years there was an apparent biblical problem about Jesus going *into* Jericho (Luke 18:35) versus Jesus *leaving* Jericho (Matthew 20:29) when He healed the blind in that vicinity. Archaeology has identified both the old and new cities, explaining the apparent contradiction. It seems Jesus was leaving the old city and was on His way to the new city when the blind beggar was healed. Many structures have been excavated in the new city of Jericho, including one of the three winter palaces of Herod the Great. Finds include coins and other artifacts that fit precisely with the historian Josephus' account that, after Herod's death, the palace was burned and then magnificently rebuilt.[3,4,5,6]

P **Jericho: The Tree of Zacchaeus**—Zacchaeus, a tax collector of short stature, climbed a sycamore tree to see Jesus in Jericho (Luke 19:1-10). Zacchaeus later became a disciple when he repented while Jesus dined at his home. A problem with this account seemed to exist since Jericho was originally believed to be only the old site (see above), which was packed with buildings and had little room for and no evidence of sycamore trees. Later excavation of the newer Jericho, however, indicated plenty of room for parks and trees. In fact, sycamore trees are still common there today.[3]

P **Jericho: The Inn of the Good Samaritan**—One of Jesus' parables tells of a "man going from Jerusalem to Jericho" who was beaten, stripped, and left by robbers. A good Samaritan helped this stranger in trouble, after more esteemed religious leaders passed him by (Luke 10:30-37). An Inn of the Good Samaritan formerly existed at the site where Jesus supposedly taught this lesson. Early writers, including Eusebius and Jerome mentioned the site where Jesus spoke the parable. A large castle was constructed there and its ruins are visible at the site today.[3]

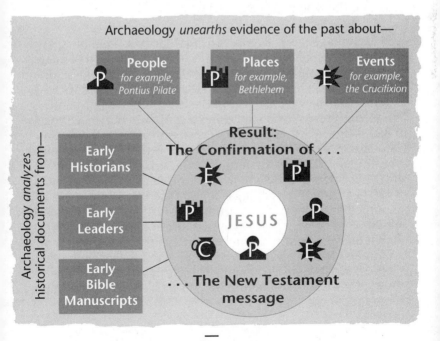

Archaeology *unearths* evidence of the past about—

People for example, Pontius Pilate

Places for example, Bethlehem

Events for example, the Crucifixion

Archaeology *analyzes* historical documents from—

Early Historians

Early Leaders

Early Bible Manuscripts

Result: The Confirmation of . . .

JESUS

. . . The New Testament message

Ancient Discoveries—
The Time of Jesus' Later Ministry

P **Bethany: The Tomb of Lazarus**—One of the most significant events of Jesus' later ministry was His raising of Lazarus from the dead (John 11) at Bethany. It was so important that it caused the Jewish leaders to immediately plot Jesus' death. Not surprisingly, the location of this event has been venerated since early times. Several early writers record the existence of the crypt of Lazarus. Excavation of the village of Bethany reveals an abundance of artifacts from the time of Christ, including many household objects, pottery samples, and coins. One part of Bethany is honeycombed with tombs, one of which has been identified as the tomb of Lazarus. Several things lead many archaeologists to believe it is authentic. First, the identification of the village and the general site is accepted. Second, the artifacts found are consistent with the period. Third, there is substantial evidence that contemporaries to the event believed this to be the actual site of the tomb. The evidence includes early graffiti written by Christians. The graffiti refer to Lazarus being raised from the dead there and request similar mercy for the writers themselves.[3,5]

P **Bethphage: Jesus Begins the Final Entry**—The Bible speaks of Jesus' late ministry involving visits to Bethphage and Bethany. Archaeology confirms that both cities lay on the side of the Mount of Olives. During Jesus' final days, He apparently resided in Bethany (Matthew 21:17). Just before His triumphal entry into Jerusalem, He sent His disciples ahead of Him to obtain a donkey in Bethphage (Matthew 21:1,2). Several early church leaders and historians give details about the village of Bethphage, including the specific place where Jesus mounted the donkey and the route by which He entered Jerusalem. Bernard the Frankish, a monk, wrote in 870 of a church containing a block of marble, using which Jesus "mounted the colt of an ass." During excavations in 1876, a cube-shaped block of stone was uncovered together with a Crusader church that was built to commemorate both the resurrection of Lazarus and Jesus' entry into Jerusalem on a colt. Paintings depicting these events were also found. Perhaps this stone, now preserved in the Chapel of Bethphage, was the actual stone Jesus used to mount the donkey.[3]

The Mount of Olives: Jesus Reveals End-Time Events—In His last days, Jesus took the disciples to a location on the Mount of Olives to tell them about the end of the world (Matthew 24:3). Eusebius, writing in the early 300s, told of a church that was erected to honor the cave where Jesus gave the end-time revelations. Excavation has located this church, which was built by Helena Augusta, Constantine's mother. The ruins of the church and cave itself, known as the "Crypt of Eleona," can be seen today. [3]

The Mount of Olives: Jesus Weeps over the City—While approaching the city, we are told, Jesus wept over it, knowing its future (Luke 19:41-44). The place of this event is now commemorated by the Franciscan Church "Dominus Flevit." The early writer and pilgrim Aetheria notes the exact route that Jesus took down the mountain. Jerome and later Middle-Ages pilgrims seem to agree on the route and on the area where Jesus dismounted from the "frisky colt" and wept over the city. [3, 5]

The Temple in Jerusalem—The most important place by far to Jews of the New Testament era was the temple. The original temple, built by Solomon in about 974 B.C., was destroyed at the time of the exile to Babylon and then was later rebuilt. King Herod the Great significantly expanded the size of the temple during his reign. Referred to by some people as the "third temple," it was destroyed in A.D. 70.

Jesus spent a significant amount of time at the temple. He was brought there to be circumcised and was blessed by prophets (Luke 2:21-38). He returned as a child for Passover celebrations (Luke 2:41). And during His ministry, Jesus certainly worshiped there and twice drove out the money changers from the temple's outer court.

Today, the location of the temple is well known (although the exact identification of its original foundations is in dispute). One of the walls from Herod's temple, the western wall, is still in existence. However, since the temple site is on Muslim-held land, in-depth study is difficult. Plans are underway to someday rebuild the temple. [3, 4,5]

P **The Last Supper**—The Last Supper is believed to have taken place in the house belonging to John Mark's mother. Other events said to have taken place there include 1) Jesus' washing of the disciples' feet (John 13:4,5); 2) the meeting of the disciples after the resurrection (Luke 24:33-49); 3) the receiving of the Holy Spirit by the disciples at Pentecost (Acts 2:1-4); and 4) the death of Jesus' mother, Mary. Early Christians identified the site and many writers later confirmed it, including Origen (in 250), Eusebius (in 300), Aetheria (in 381), Jerome (in 400), and Theodosius (in 530).

A "great church" was built on the site—located on Mount Zion only 200 "paces" from Golgotha (the site of the crucifixion of Jesus). The church was destroyed by the Persians in 614 and later rebuilt. Excavations in and around the church have located part of a first-century "synagogue" that seems to be similar to the "house-synagogue" created in the house of Peter after the resurrection. It may have been built in the house of John Mark's mother. Interestingly, a niche that was used to hold holy Scripture was oriented towards Golgotha instead of in the customary direction towards the Temple. This probably reflected a change in worship based on Jesus' once-and-for-all sacrifice. [3,5]

P **Gethsemane**—The Gethsemane Church of All Nations marks the site revered for centuries as the place where Jesus went before being betrayed. In the center of the eastern nave is a rock, identified as the very rock on which Jesus prayed (Matthew 26:36). The church is built on the foundation of an earlier Byzantine church. Eusebius identified the site in 330. [3,4,5]

P **The Trials of Jesus: Caiaphas and Pilate**—Jesus went through a series of trials centering around the house of Caiaphas, the High Priest (John 18:24), and the palace of Pilate. Although sites for both have been suggested, neither has been confirmed yet. However, first-century stone steps leading from the place of the Last Supper to Gethsemane, and from Gethsemane to the general location of the house of the High Priest, have been excavated. These steps are almost certainly the ones Jesus trod during this remarkable week in history. [3]

P **The Site of Jesus' Death and Resurrection**—The Church of the Holy Sepulchre marks the site most archaeologists agree is the place of Jesus' crucifixion and resurrection. Such a site would certainly be remembered by early Christians. So important was the site that the emperor Hadrian placed a statue of the pagan god Venus on the site of Golgotha (where Jesus was crucified) and a similar statue of Jupiter on the tomb of the resurrection, hoping that Christians would forget their holy sites. Instead it helped them mark and remember the location. (This same approach was tried by Hadrian in Bethlehem.)

Later, when Constantine ended persecution by making Christianity the state religion of Rome, his mother Helena helped erect a church over the two sites. A large gathering of bishops was held in Jerusalem to consecrate the church in the year 335. Eusebius was present and wrote about its significance. Later, in 348, Cyril of Jerusalem gave a famous series of lectures in the church, repeatedly mentioning the historical significance of the site. It was recorded that even wood from the three crosses and the sign in three languages above Jesus' head were in existence in the church at that time. Cyril also gave a vivid description of the tomb in which Jesus lay, before Constantine's workmen started construction of elaborate buildings to honor the site. (Cyril had been born early enough to see the site both before and after the church was built.)

Several other early writers also mentioned the church, Golgotha, and the tomb. Although the church suffered the destruction common to most Christian landmarks, it was repeatedly rebuilt and stands today as a silent reminder of the most important event in history.[3,4,5]

P **The Ascension of Jesus**—Jesus' last act on earth was His ascension into heaven (Luke 24:50-53; Acts 1:9). The place of this event was noted by early Christian writers (for example, Aetheria in 381), but no mention of a church was made. A Church of the Ascension did exist by the year 404, when it was described by Jerome. Destroyed by the Persians in 614, it was rebuilt by the year 670, when Arculf speaks of the "last footprints" of the Lord being visible by the light of an "eternally" burning lamp. In 1187 the church was taken over by the Muslims and turned into a mosque, which it remains today.[3, 5]

Ancient Discoveries—
The Time of Church Expansion

Various Languages Spoken at Pentecost—The disciples suddenly started speaking in various languages (tongues) at Pentecost when the Holy Spirit came upon them. The languages they spoke included ones from Phrygia, Egypt, and Rome, as well as several other places. Excavations have confirmed the presence of Jews in all of these regions early in the first century. The broad dispersion of Jews throughout the Mediterranean area would explain why there were so many Jewish people who spoke foreign languages among those who had come to Jerusalem for the holy feasts[1] (Acts 2:6-12).

Deception by Sapphira—Sapphira and her husband lied to the Holy Spirit about their gift to the early church, resulting in their sudden judgment and death. It had been called into question as to whether the name "Sapphira" was a legitimate first-century name, until several ossuaries and other sites containing the name were discovered in 1933[1] (Acts 5:1).

The Synagogue of the Freedmen—Members of the "Synagogue of the Freedmen" spoke against Stephen but could not stand up against his wisdom and the Spirit. This reference remained a mystery until excavation in Jerusalem in 1913 revealed an inscription of the name "Theodotus" as the builder of a synagogue. This inscription revealed that Theodotus' father was one of the Jews captured by the Roman general Pompey and later liberated—hence becoming one of the "freedmen"[1] (Acts 6:9).

The Ethiopian Eunuch—After the resurrection, the apostle Philip met an Ethiopian eunuch—an "important official in charge of all the treasury of Candace, queen of the Ethiopians." Excavations in Nubia revealed evidence of a series of queens called Candace. Ethiopian queens were still referred to as "Candace" as late as the first century[1] (Acts 8:26-40).

Confirmation of the Existence of Sergius Paulus—Sergius Paulus, a Roman proconsul, wanted to hear the Word of God, so he sent for Paul and Barnabas. Excavations in his city, Paphos on the island of Cyprus, revealed inscriptions of the names Sergius Paulus and Sergia Paula, children of a "commissioner." These are believed to be the son and daughter of the Sergius Paulus mentioned in the Bible. Further research reveals that the daughter may have been instructing her children in the Christian faith and that her husband may have left public service because he had become a Christian[1] (Acts 13:6-12).

🔆 **John Mark's Sudden Return to Jerusalem**—One event that has been a puzzle for Christian scholars is John Mark's (Paul's companion) sudden return to Jerusalem during Paul's first missionary journey (Acts 13:13). This upset Paul greatly and caused him to refuse to work with John Mark on his second trip (Acts 15:38,39). Some scholars have suggested that John Mark was homesick, others that he was ill or that he resented the change of leadership from Barnabas (his cousin) to Paul. Archaeology has identified another potentially more reasonable cause. While in Asia Minor, Paul and Barnabas decided to continue on from Perga to Antioch in Pisidia. Many ancient inscriptions have been found referring to the extreme danger of bandits in that area and the need for policemen and soldiers. Paul refers to this kind of danger in his letter to the Corinthians (2 Corinthians 11:26). Perhaps John Mark chose not to face such danger.[1]

> ### The Conversion of Paul—Skeptics Ask Why
> (Acts 9)
>
> Saul (later Paul) was widely known among the Jews as a Pharisee and an avid persecutor of Christians. Upon seeing the risen Christ, Paul was struck blind—and then was healed exactly as Jesus had prophesied. Paul then gave up wealth and prestige in exchange for a life of great suffering and eventually a painful death. He started many new churches and wrote more of the New Testament than anyone else. History supports these facts. Skeptics wonder why Paul did this.

Correction of Information About Iconium, Lystra, and Derbe—Luke tells of Paul and Barnabas leaving the city of Iconium and traveling on to Lystra and Derbe in the region of Lycaonia, thus implying that Iconium was not in the same region as the other two cities. This contradicts several Roman writers (including Cicero), who indicate the three cities were all in Lycaonia. Hence historians concluded the Bible was in error. The archaeologist Sir William Ramsay located a monument in 1910 in Asia Minor that showed Iconium was indeed not in Lycaonia, but was in Phrygia. Further discoveries brought to light the fact that Iconians prided themselves upon being citizens of a Phrygian city—all of which clearly verifies Luke's accuracy—and corrects the Roman writers[1](Acts 14:6).

Confirmation of the "District" of Macedonia—Luke refers to the city of Philippi as being in the "district" (*meris* in Greek) of Macedonia. A well-known New Testament scholar, F. J. A. Hort, declared that Luke was wrong, since the Greek word *meris*, which Luke used, "never denotes a region or other such geographical division." Excavations in the Egyptian colony of Fayam, which was founded by Philippians, have turned up the use of exactly the same wording as Luke's to describe the geographical divisions of the colony. Archaeology again confirms that the accuracy of the Bible is superior to the knowledge of today's recognized experts[1] (Acts 16:12).

Confirmation of the Word "Rulers"—Luke referrs to the rulers of the city of Thessalonica (in Macedonia) as *politarchs*. This also was thought to be in error until seventeen ancient inscriptions that support Luke's choice of this word were discovered in the modern city of Thessaloniki[1] (Acts 17:6,8).

Paul's Stay in Corinth—Paul's eighteen-month stay in Corinth was second only to his stay in Ephesus in duration (Acts 18:11). His choice to remain there was undoubtedly influenced by the importance of Corinth as a center for business and athletics, which caused great numbers of people to pass through its gates. Extensive archaeological study reveals what the city was like in Paul's day. In the city center was a great *agora* (a public square and marketplace—the hub of activity in any Greek city). Here, overlooking a 600-foot long by 300-foot wide area, was a platform used by public officials to make judicial decisions or address large crowds. No doubt Paul stood before Gallio, the regional proconsul, in this same place (Acts 18:12,13). Near the entrance to the agora, a stone was unearthed that bears the inscription "the Synagogue of the Hebrews." Many scholars believe this to be the door lintel of the synagogue in which Paul preached (Acts 18:4).[1]

Inscription Naming Erastus—The 14,000 seat theater at Corinth contains an inscription in the pavement near the stage indicating that "Erastus" laid the pavement "at his own expense." This Erastus is believed to be the same one Paul referred to in his letter to the Romans (Romans 16:23), which was drafted when he was in Corinth. Erastus was the city's "director of public works."[1]

The Dating of the Book of Revelation—Some scholars have questioned the dating of the book of Revelation. They have proposed that its rather unusual usage of Greek combined with Hebrew word construction indicates John wrote it before he had written the Gospel of John—before he had learned Greek well. However, several archaeological discoveries of papyri (in Egypt) have shown that the supposed "bad grammar" was actually the common manner of expression in that area and period. These and other papyri make clear that the *Koine* Greek written and spoken by many Jews of John's time was not only influenced by their native Aramaic language, but was also colored with many Hellenistic expressions current in the entire eastern Mediterranean region.

Yet another attempt at redating the book was made by Nikolaus Morosow, who proposed that Revelation had been written as an astrological exercise by John Chrysostom in the year 395. However, a nearly perfect copy of Revelation discovered in Egypt that dates back to the fourth century indicates that the book was in broad circulation by that time. The best evidence leads us to rely on writings by several early church fathers that point to a date of authorship of about A.D. 95.[1]

Common Questions

What If I Don't Believe the Entire Bible?

Having a relationship with God does not depend on believing the entire Bible. Belief in and acceptance of Jesus as Savior are all that is required. Those who thoroughly investigate the Bible find abundant evidence that every claim of the Bible is true—and nearly all claims have substantial support. Even when "modern" science seems at odds with it, the Bible has ultimately proven true. But waiting to accept a relationship with Christ until *all* doubts are answered would be foolish. Your time on earth could end tomorrow. Instead, pray for insight. The truth will eventually be revealed.

How Can We Ensure the Right Relationship to Go to Heaven?

When Jesus said not all who use His name will enter heaven (Matthew 7:21–23), He was referring to people who think using Christ's name along with rituals and rules is the key to heaven. A *relationship* with God is *not* based on rituals and rules. It's based on grace and forgiveness—and the right kind of relationship with Him.

How to Have a Personal Relationship with God

1. **B***elieve that God exists* and that He came to earth in the human form of Jesus Christ (John 3:16; Romans 10:9).

2. **A***ccept God's free forgiveness* of sins through the death and resurrection of Jesus Christ (Ephesians 2:8-10; 1:7,8).

3. **S***witch to God's plan for life* (1 Peter 1:21-23; Ephesians 2:1-5).

4. **E***xpress desire for Christ to be director of your life* (Matthew 7:21-27; 1 John 4:15).

Prayer for Eternal Life with God

"Dear God, I believe You sent Your Son, Jesus, to die for my sins so I can be forgiven. I'm sorry for my sins, and I want to live the rest of my life the way You want me to. Please put Your Spirit in my life to direct me. Amen."

Then What?

People who sincerely take the above steps automatically become members of God's family of believers. A new world of freedom and strength is available through prayer and obedience to God's will. New members of God's family can build their relationship with God by taking the following steps:

- Find a Bible-based church that you like and attend regularly.

- Try to set aside some time each day to pray and read the Bible.

- Locate other Christians to spend time with on a regular basis.

God's Promises to Believers

For Today

But seek first His kingdom and His righteousness, and all these things [things to satisfy all your needs] will be given to you as well.
—Matthew 6:33

For Eternity

Whoever believes in the Son has eternal life, but whoever rejects the Son will not see life, for God's wrath remains on him.
—John 3:36

Once we develop an eternal perspective, even the greatest problems on earth fade in significance.

Notes

1. Free, Joseph P., and Vos, Howard F., *Archaeology and Bible History*, Grand Rapids, MI: Zondervan Publishing House, 1992.

2. Millard, Alan, *Illustrated Wonders & Discoveries of the Bible*, Nashville, TN: Thomas Nelson, Inc., 1997.

3. Finegan, Jack, *The Archeology of the New Testament*, Princeton, NJ: Princeton University Press, 1992.

4. *Historical Geography Notebook*, Mount Zion, Jerusalem, Israel: Jerusalem University College, Institute of Holy Land Studies.

5. McRay, John, *Archaeology & the New Testament*, Grand Rapids, MI: Baker Book House, 1991.

6. Josephus, Flavius, *The Complete Works of Josephus*, Grand Rapids, MI: Kregel Publications, 1981.

Bibliography

Archeology and the Bible, The Best of BAR, Volume II: Archaeology in the World of Herod, Jesus and Paul, Washington, DC: Bible Archaeology Society, 1990.

Eerdman's Handbook to the Bible, Littlemore, Oxford, England: Lion Publishing, 1973.

The Harper Atlas of the Bible, New York, NY: Harper & Row, 1987.

Jeffrey, Grant R., *The Signature of God*, Toronto, Ontario, Canada: Frontier Research Publications, 1996.

Life Application Bible, Wheaton, IL: Tyndale House Publishers, and Grand Rapids, MI: Zondervan Publishing House, 1991.

McDowell, Josh, *Evidence that Demands a Verdict—Vol. I*, Nashville, TN: Thomas Nelson, Inc., 1979.

McDowell, Josh, *Evidence that Demands a Verdict—Vol. II*, Nashville, TN: Thomas Nelson, Inc., 1993.

McDowell, Josh, and Wilson, Bill, *A Ready Defense*, San Bernardino, CA: Here's Life Publishers, Inc., 1990.

Muncaster, Ralph O., *The Bible—Prophecy Miracles—Investigation of the Evidence*, Mission Viejo, CA: Strong Basis to Believe, 1996.

Nelson's Complete Book of Bible Maps & Charts, Nashville, TN: Thomas Nelson, Inc., 1996.

Packer, J.I., Tenney, Merrill C., and White, William Jr., *Illustrated Encyclopedia of Bible Facts*, Nashville, TN: Thomas Nelson, Inc., 1980.

Price, Randall, *Secrets of the Dead Sea Scrolls*, Eugene, OR: Harvest House Publishers, 1996.

Shanks, Hershel (editor), *Understanding the Dead Sea Scrolls*, New York, NY: Vintage Books, 1993.

Scott, Julius J., PhD, *Life and Teachings of Jesus*, Audio tape, Wheaton, IL: Wheaton College Graduate School Extension Studies, 1988.

Smith, F. LaGard, *The Daily Bible in Chronological Order*, Eugene, OR: Harvest House Publishers, 1984.

Unger, Merrill F., *The New Unger's Bible Handbook*, Chicago, IL: Moody Press, 1984.

Vos, Howard F., *Introduction to Church History*, Nashville, TN: Nelson, 1994.

Youngblood, Ronald F., *New Illustrated Bible Dictionary*, Nashville, TN: Nelson, 1995.

What the Bible is All About—Quick Reference Edition, Ventura, CA: Regal Books, 1989.

Who's Who in the Bible, Pleasantville, NY: Reader's Digest, 1994.